Frozen
BEGINNINGS

Elsa's Icy Rescue

By Kate Egan

Illustrated By
Mario Cortes

SCHOLASTIC
SYDNEY AUCKLAND NEW YORK TORONTO LONDON MEXICO CITY
NEW DELHI HONG KONG BUENOS AIRES PUERTO RICO

Published by Scholastic Australia in 2021.

Scholastic Australia Pty Limited
PO Box 579 Gosford NSW 2250
ABN 11 000 614 577
www.scholastic.com.au

Part of the Scholastic Group
Sydney • Auckland • New York • Toronto • London • Mexico City
New Delhi • Hong Kong • Buenos Aires • Puerto Rico

ISBN 978-1-76112-575-1

Printed in China.

Scholastic Australia's policy, in association with its printers, is to use papers that are renewable and made efficiently from wood grown in responsibly managed forests, so as to minimise its environmental footprint.

10 9 8 7 6 5 4 3 2 1 21 22 23 24 25 / 2

Chapter 1
The Sommerhus

As the royal carriage made its way past rows of tall pines, Elsa felt far from home. All she could hear was the steady *clomp, clomp* of the white horses' hooves and the call of distant birds. Oh, yes, and the voice of her little sister, Anna. 'Are we there yet?' Anna asked every few minutes. 'Are we almost there?'

It was summertime and Elsa's family were making their annual trip to the Sommerhus, a quaint cottage in a small village just outside the Arendelle forest. Every summer, they left the castle behind and stayed a few weeks alone at the cottage, without castle staff or royal responsibilities.

Back home in Arendelle, Elsa spent every day preparing for the distant future when she would become queen. She spent hours with the castle governess in the schoolroom, reviewing the names of past rulers and going over royal etiquette. At the Sommerhus, though, she did not have to think about her future at all. While they were away, they could be just a normal family and Elsa could be just a normal girl.

Elsa's mother, Queen Iduna, looked out the window as the carriage passed another row of trees outside. She breathed in deeply and said, 'Don't you love the smell of cedar?'

'I think we're almost there!' Anna cried. She twisted towards the carriage window and pointed at a path paved with pebbles. 'Yes, this is where we turn!'

Elsa's father, King Agnarr, extended his arm to make sure Anna didn't tumble out the window. 'It's still a little further,' he said. 'Just be patient—we'll be there in no time.'

Catching her sister's eye, Elsa smiled.

Who could be patient when they were getting so close?

Her mind raced, thinking about everything their trip would hold. Elsa loved the feeling of being alone with her family at the edge of the forest. She looked forward to all their summer traditions—playing games and making music and hiking through the hills. There would be new adventures too, of course, and Elsa could only wonder what they would be.

The carriage pitched forwards as it went over a bump in the road. Suddenly, Elsa knew just where they were. 'This is it!' she said, leaning across the carriage to hug her sister as the road wound past a wooden stave church in a tiny village. She knew every inch of the rest of the way.

They went around another bend, moving through the town square and approaching a cobblestone path. At the end of the road, Elsa could see their cheerful cottage, with its sturdy log walls and bright red trim. The window boxes were planted with pink and white flowers and the grass was freshly cut. The Sommerhus was just as friendly and welcoming as Elsa remembered it.

As soon as the carriage stopped, the girls leaped out and ran to the heavy front door. Anna pushed and pushed, but she couldn't get it open until Elsa stepped up beside her to lend an extra hand. 'One, two, three!' the sisters counted. And the door to their summer adventures swung wide open.

Elsa stepped into the cottage and circled around, taking it all in.

First she saw the long wooden table where her family would gather for their meals. Behind it was a grandfather clock that had belonged to Elsa's own grandfather and the large fireplace that warmed the cottage when the nights grew cool. In every corner, there were stacks of favourite books and games. On a narrow shelf near the ceiling were the beautiful plates Elsa's mother had collected on her travels as queen. And hanging on the wall were the fiddles her father played in the evening. Everything was just as she remembered.

Elsa grabbed Anna by the hand and pulled her up the stairs, taking them two at a time. 'Let's go see our room!' she said.

At the cottage, Anna and Elsa shared a room under the eaves. It was small and dark and some nights they could hear the sound of raindrops pounding against the roof. This was where Elsa had her happiest dreams.

Elsa walked into the room and stretched out on her bed. On the other side of the room, Anna bounced on her mattress. 'Let's go exploring!' she said.

But Elsa was not ready to explore. She wanted to soak in the feeling of being inside the Sommerhus at last. Fortunately, she knew something that would keep Anna occupied for a little while. 'Not yet,' she said. 'But look at this.'

On Elsa's side of the room was a small wooden trunk with pink trim. She hopped off her bed, crouched and lifted the lid, its hinges squeaking.

Inside the trunk were the toys the girls

played with only at the Sommerhus. Eight-year-old Elsa had nearly outgrown the building blocks and spinning tops, but there were some toys she would never get too old for. Tucked carefully at the bottom of the trunk, covered with soft blankets, was a pair of well-loved dolls. Elsa lifted one out as if it was an old friend. The doll had blonde braids and bright blue eyes. Elsa hugged it and said, 'Good to see you, Hildy!'

'Hanna! Hanna!' Anna cried, edging her sister out of the way. She pulled the other doll from the trunk and lifted it into the air. 'We're back!' This doll had red hair the same shade as Anna's. Anna lifted Hildy from Elsa's arms. In no time, she was changing both dolls into their summer dresses.

Returning to her bed and lying back on her pillow, Elsa sighed and smiled.

Elsa would miss some things about the castle while they were gone, of course, but the Sommerhus felt like home to her. Not only was it the place she got to spend time with her family and take a break from her lessons, but it was where she could be herself—her *whole* self. At the Sommerhus, she didn't have to hide her magic.

Since she'd been there last, Elsa had learned more about her astonishing power. Whenever she wanted, she could create ice and snow. Well . . . sort of. Until she knew how to use her power properly, she had to keep it out of sight. At the Sommerhus, no-one outside the family would see her—and no-one would stop her—so she could test the limits of her magic.

Chapter 2
A Walk in the Woods

'After you finish unpacking, who's ready for a walk to the fjord?' Queen Iduna called from downstairs. The sisters were putting their clothes and bags away. The dolls, Hildy and Hanna, waited patiently on the windowsill.

'We're ready right now!' Elsa called back. The sisters hurried down the steps to join their mother.

The sky was blue and the sun bright as Anna and Elsa followed their parents into the afternoon. A trip to the sparkling fjord was always a highlight of the family's first day away from home.

Queen Iduna led the way behind the cottage and to a hidden path near the edge of the forest. The path wove around some tall trees and soon the cottage was out of sight. The family was alone with the wonders of nature.

Elsa wondered what people in Arendelle would say if they could see their queen right then. Her mother was practically skipping along the path. 'I can't wait to put my toes in the water,' she said. Elsa giggled. Her mother sounded like Anna.

Her father was watching the sky intently. 'Could that be a hawk?' he wondered aloud, pointing at something as it swooped overhead. Not many people knew that the king had a special interest in birds.

The grassy path gave way to a rougher trail studded with stones, leading up a gentle incline. As the family climbed higher, there were some larger rocks in their way. Anna and Elsa raced around them and soon the girls were ahead of their parents.

'Don't touch the ground!' Anna dared Elsa. This was one of their favourite games.

Instead of stepping directly on the trail, the girls hopped from stone to stone. If there were no stones, they walked on roots or tree stumps or clumps of leaves—anything to avoid the ground.

Anna reached a stretch of trail with nothing else to step on. The only way to avoid the ground was to swing from a tree branch like a monkey.

When Elsa got to that same part of the trail, she decided to do something else. Sure, she could swing like a monkey . . . or she could avoid the ground in her *own* way.

Elsa looked around to make sure no-one outside her family was around. Then she stretched out her hands and waved them over the path. She could feel her magic building, but she never quite knew what was about to happen. Would it work? Elsa held her breath. But in no time, the ground was covered by a thin sheet of ice about as long as she was tall

and Elsa could walk right on it. Success!

Anna looked back and saw the ice glinting in a patch of sunlight. 'No fair!' she said. 'That's against the rules!' But Anna also saw the possibility for fun. She raced towards Elsa and took a flying leap onto the ice, gliding from one end to the other.

'Too bad I don't have my ice skates,' Anna said. There wasn't enough ice for skating, but as Elsa slid to the edge of the ice and continued on, she wondered if she could make more next time.

By the time their parents came up the trail, the thin layer of ice had melted to a trickle in the heat and the girls had scrambled even further ahead. Elsa was near the top of the hill when she heard her mother's voice through the trees.

'Anna! Elsa!' she called.

Soon her father chimed in. 'Wherever you are, stop and wait for us!'

It was only a few minutes before King Agnarr and Queen Iduna reached their daughters, but the king seemed worried. 'Please don't get too far ahead,' he said. 'It's important that we all stay together for safety's sake.'

Just ahead, the trail ended at a bluff. The whole family walked together until they reached the very best view in the kingdom. From the top of the bluff, they could see a wide vista of shining blue water, with snow-covered mountains in the distance. The fjord was dotted with colourful boats and a few rocky islands covered in pine. Elsa took a deep breath. There was no place she would rather be.

The queen scrambled down the bluff towards the water and the sandy shore, calling 'Follow me!' It was tradition for the girls and their mother to wade into the

water before the end of their first day at the Sommerhus.

Quickly, the three of them took off their shoes and dipped in their feet. 'Too cold!' said Anna, running away from the water as soon as she felt its bite. Elsa waded in up to her ankles. She didn't mind the chill one bit.

After the dip in the water, Elsa and Anna made sand angels near the shore until it was time to go back to the cottage. Their mother led the way down the trail but stopped short. 'Oh, how wonderful!' she cried, crouching in front of a bush. 'Girls, come and see!' She plucked fresh strawberries off the bush and dropped them into her daughters' outstretched hands. 'Nature feeds our spirits *and* our bodies,' she told Elsa and Anna.

'Look, there are more!' Elsa said, venturing away from the trail and into the forest. She could see many more strawberry bushes growing in the shadows.

But her father put a hand on her elbow. 'Remember, Elsa. We need to stay together. There could be dangers hidden in the forest.'

Elsa stepped back so as not to worry her father. With her power, though, came a growing confidence. Whatever dangers came her way, she would always have a means to face them.

Chapter 3
Building the Fort

That night, Elsa and Anna pushed their beds next to each other and curled up together under one big blanket. Elsa loved the cosy feeling of sleeping next to her sister. The only tricky part was the morning. At the castle, Anna could sleep all day if their parents let her. But at the Sommerhus, no matter how late she went to bed, Anna always woke up early. She was too excited to stay asleep!

So it was no surprise when Anna started tugging Elsa's arm at the faintest sign of dawn the next day. 'Elsa!' she whispered. 'Time to get up!'

Elsa pulled a pillow over her eyes and shrank beneath the blanket. Then she felt a gust of cold air as Anna peeled the blanket off her legs.

'Want to play?' Anna asked. 'I have a great idea!'

Elsa sat up and hit her head on the low ceiling. 'It's too early!' she said, rubbing her head.

'But we have to make a fort!' Anna explained. 'I have it all figured out. I just need you to help me set it up.'

'What do we need a fort for?' Elsa asked, yawning.

'It's for Hildy and Hanna!' Anna said. 'They need a Sommerhus of their own.'

Elsa fell back on the bed. It was impossible to say no to Anna, because she would continue to ask and ask until she got what she wanted. The first ray of sunshine pierced the room as Elsa sat up again, blinking. 'Where do you think we should put it?'

Anna grinned and replied, 'Right here.' She patted the bed and gestured to a large blanket she had found that they could use for the fort's roof.

Elsa dragged some chairs over and placed them on either side of the two twin beds. Anna draped the blanket on top of them and for a minute it was perfect—until the blanket began to sag. 'I think we need to tie the blanket to the chairs,' Elsa said. 'That way it will stay put.'

The girls knotted the blanket to the chairs with hair ribbons and pulled it tight, but the knots had a way of loosening after a few minutes. Could Elsa use her magic to fix this problem? After a few moments of intense concentration, she conjured up some bits of ice and froze the blanket to the chairs. Problem solved—at least until the ice melted.

'Watch out,' Anna cautioned as she carried a pile of pillows across the room. From inside the fort, Elsa watched Anna stagger towards her, pillows teetering in her arms. They fell just as she reached the fort. Elsa crawled out, giggling, and took the pillows into the fort one by one.

'Hanna and Hildy are going to love it in here!' Elsa told her sister. But the fort wasn't only for the dolls, Elsa knew. She and Anna were going to love it in there, too. And the best part was that they had all day to play.

The only thing that could drag them out of the fort was the sound of their father's voice downstairs. 'Time for breakfast!' he called.

By the time Elsa had gotten to her feet, Anna was already halfway down the stairs. Back home in Arendelle, King Agnarr never made breakfast. On their summer trip, though, he made pancakes every morning and he had promised their favourite: pancakes with chocolate.

The long table was set with a purple tablecloth and a vase of wildflowers from their walk the day before. There was a pitcher of cold milk and a bottle of syrup that glowed like gold. Best of all, Elsa thought, one of her mother's special plates sat at each place.

Usually the plates were kept on a shelf, but they came out for important occasions, like their first breakfast together at the Sommerhus. Each plate was a memento from their parents' travels around the kingdom.

Elsa sat at the table. She picked up one of

her favourite plates—painted with a crocus—and flopped a pancake on top.

No-one could see the design on Anna's plate because pancakes covered every inch. They were piled high and overflowing off the edge and Anna splashed syrup over them with such force that drops flew across the table. When she poured her milk, some of it missed the glass and ended up on the floor.

'Elsa,' her mother cautioned. Startled, Elsa looked up. Had her mother mixed up the sisters? Sometimes she did that, calling one by the other's name. In spite of Anna's mess, though, the queen was looking at *her.*

‘Remember where to leave your knife after you cut your pancakes,’ her mother said. ‘It should rest on the side of your plate, not on the table.’

Elsa looked at Anna, who was picking up a pancake with her fingers. Did her mother even notice?

‘A future queen must watch her manners,’ Queen Iduna said. ‘That will be our project for today.’

‘We already have a project for today,’ Anna announced. ‘Wait until you see our fort.’

Queen Iduna shook her head. ‘I’m afraid things will be a little different this year,’ she said. ‘Now that Elsa is getting older, we are going to keep up her lessons while we’re here.’

Elsa swallowed her last bite, though the pancake didn’t taste quite as sweet anymore. *This isn’t fair!* she thought. Their summer trip was the only time she didn’t have to think about becoming queen.

What was the point of a trip with her

family, Elsa wondered, if she would have to sit through all the same lessons she had at home? She wouldn't get to spend the morning playing with Anna after all. And not even her magic could change that.

Chapter 4
Lessons for Elsa

Anna gave Elsa a hug when she finished breakfast. 'I won't play in the fort until you can come, too,' she promised. Her syrupy hands stuck to Elsa's hair when she pulled away.

Elsa managed a small smile. 'It's okay,' she told her sister. 'The lessons will fly by.'

One of the first rules of being a ruler

was never to complain about ruling. But Elsa was disappointed.

While her father and Anna walked to the village, Elsa and her mother settled down in two big chairs in front of the fireplace. It was sunny outside, but a chill hung over the room.

Queen Iduna cleared her throat. 'Let's get started by reviewing some of the material your teacher gave me to go over with you,' she said, consulting the large book in her lap. 'Do you remember the first ten rulers of Arendelle?'

Just like her routine back home, the day's

lessons started with a little history. Usually, Elsa did her lessons with her governess, Miss Larsen, but her mum had explained that she would be taking over Elsa's teaching while they were away. After all, her mum had taken the same lessons before she had become queen many years before and who

better to teach Elsa how to be a proper ruler than the current queen of Arendelle?

Elsa kept her voice steady as she recited the past kings and queens. It was a long list of names, but Elsa remembered every single one.

'Very good!' Queen Iduna said when she was finished. 'Shall we move on to the national treasures?'

Dutifully, Elsa described the national treasures of the kingdom. They were crowns and jewelled sceptres, ceremonial robes and special books that had been important to the family for centuries.

'Well done!' her mother said. 'Soon, you

will be ready to visit the vault where they are kept.'

Elsa did not want to visit the vault. She did not want to do anything except finish the lesson. None of this was how she had imagined her time at the Sommerhus. But she knew that complaining would only make the lessons longer.

Queen Iduna seemed to sense Elsa's disinterest. After reviewing a few more national treasures, she said, 'Let's finish today's lessons with something new and review proper place settings and table manners.'

Her mother stood up and led the way back to the table where they had eaten breakfast. Thanks to King Agnarr, the mess had disappeared and the plates were neatly stacked after washing.

Queen Iduna took a clean plate off the top of the stack and laid it on the table in front of Elsa. 'A formal meal is different from a family meal,' she began. 'First, let me show you how a place setting should look.'

Elsa nodded.

'The plate is at the centre,' the queen said. Then she showed Elsa the proper place for everything else that would surround it on a table, from the napkin to the dessert plate. Elsa did not know there was supposed to be a special plate for dessert!

Forks, knives, spoons, glasses – Elsa knew what all those were used for. For a formal occasion, though, it turned out each place setting needed three forks, three spoons and something called a finger bowl. 'It will be filled with water,' her mother explained. 'And before dessert, your guests will dip their fingertips in to clean them.'

'Like a bath?' Elsa asked. 'Just for your fingers?'

Her mother smiled. 'Exactly like a bath. But only for fingertips. First one hand and then the other, but never the whole hand.' Elsa bit her lip to keep from laughing. It all sounded so silly.

'And of course,' Queen Iduna added, winking, 'one must never drink the water. That is considered terribly rude.'

The idea of someone drinking the finger-bowl water made Elsa crack up. 'Like drinking from the bathtub?' she said, giggling.

Her mother ruffled her hair a little. 'Just like that,' she said. 'See how much you have already learned today?'

Elsa frowned. She knew her mother was right, but there was so much more that Elsa needed to know.

Finally, she asked, 'But why? Why do I

need to know the names and the treasures and the rules? What makes the crown jewels so special, or the place settings so important? Who were all of these kings and queens, anyway?'

Queen Iduna replied, 'Well, that is the best part of preparing to be queen. Learning the stories of our people.'

'But I don't know any of the stories!' Elsa insisted. 'I only know the lists and the rules.'

Her mother gave her a patient smile. She unstacked some more plates and placed them on the table in front of her, all in a row. 'The stories are in everything we do, Elsa,' she said. 'Even on these plates. They hold memories of my travels, yes. But also memories that are passed from one generation to the next.'

She pointed to the plate Elsa's pancake had been on, now clean. 'This crocus is the crest of our kingdom, the symbol of rebirth after a long winter.' Elsa had never really thought about the crest before, but she knew the joy of seeing spring's first blossoms.

The next plate showed bright lights in a dark sky and Queen Iduna said, 'The day your papa's parents were married, the northern lights blazed overhead, just like

this. It was a good omen for their reign. This picture shows that bit of history.'

Elsa had never heard that detail, but she liked it.

There was a giant white bunny on the next plate, bigger than any Elsa had ever seen. 'And here is the mythical snow hare, said to bring good luck to those who can catch him. But he is tricky,' the queen said, 'so his good luck can be hard to find. Arendelle has many legends like this one.'

Elsa studied history every day, but she had never thought of it this way before. It was about facts, yes, but also about stories and legends.

Just then, she heard her father and Anna coming up the path from the village. Her father was walking slowly, scanning the sky for birds. Anna was doing a series of cartwheels. How long had they been gone? The morning had passed quickly after all.

Elsa had wanted to skip her lessons so she could play with her sister and experiment with her magic. But there was another reason, too, one she didn't like to admit.

Sometimes Elsa was nervous about becoming queen. With her power, she knew she'd be unlike any queen Arendelle had ever known and learning how to use a finger bowl would not make a difference.

But what if her mother's stories would help Elsa understand her place in the kingdom? Those were lessons she could use—and they could last a lifetime.

Chapter 5
Elsa's Mistake

The next few mornings at the Sommerhus followed the same routine as the first. After breakfast, Elsa would join her mother for lessons while Anna and King Agnarr would go play outside.

At the end of every lesson, Queen Iduna would take out one of her special plates and tell Elsa the story that went along with it. The stories almost made Elsa forget about the playtime she was missing with Anna. Almost.

Just as Queen Iduna finished telling Elsa the legend of a horse made of water, Anna burst into the cottage like a tornado. She told Elsa about every animal and flower she'd seen on her walk, barely pausing to catch a breath as she led Elsa upstairs.

Standing in the doorway of the bedroom, Anna narrowed her eyes and looked critically at the fort. 'I think we should make it bigger,' she told Elsa.

Elsa found extra chairs and blankets in their parents' room. She dragged the chairs to the fort and re-draped the blankets to fit. The new fort was so big that it went beyond their beds and took up almost the girls' entire room!

Anna crouched and went inside. 'We need supplies,' she said.

'What kind of supplies?' Elsa asked.

Anna thought for a moment. 'Art supplies. Some toys. And definitely sweets.'

In one corner of the fort, they piled paper and quills in case they wanted to draw pictures. They created a place for toys and books. Anna flopped on her back and announced, 'I think we can stay here all summer!'

Hildy and Hanna, their beloved dolls, had a corner of the fort to themselves. Anna made sure each one had a place to sleep, then Elsa remembered a tea set that was buried in the trunk. 'Maybe Hildy and Hanna need a place for tea,' she said.

Together, the sisters fashioned a table and chairs from a book and two small cushions. But when Elsa uncovered the tea set from the depths of the trunk, she found that the cups and saucers were chipped and coated with dust. Frowning, she told Anna, 'Hanna and Hildy deserve better than this. I know something they will like much more.'

Elsa hurried downstairs and back to the table, slipping two plates—the crocus and the snow hare—off the top of the stack. Her parents had not seen or heard her take them, since they were walking in the garden.

The family would not need *every* plate at each meal, Elsa told herself as she returned to Anna. Okay, she was not sure she was allowed to play with them. But these plates were special to the whole family, Elsa reasoned. And if the plates were in the fort, she could tell Anna what she had learned about them. Surely, her mother would be okay with that. On top of the plates, Elsa placed a pair of teacups for the dolls.

Back in the fort, Anna had propped Hildy and Hanna in sitting positions on their beds. Elsa gave each doll a teacup and a plate, then a couple of sweets from the kitchen. She swatted away Anna's hand as it snaked towards the treats. 'Those are for Hildy and Hanna!' Elsa said.

Anna made a face, but she dropped her hand. Then she poured pretend tea into each cup. Anna acted like she was taking a sip, then blew cool air over the top. 'Oh, that's too hot for you,' she told the dolls. 'You'll need to wait till it cools.'

'Or maybe not,' said Elsa. She smiled at her sister as an idea came to her. 'After all,

I happen to be an expert in ice.'

She stretched out her hands. She closed her eyes and concentrated and when she opened them, there was a misshapen piece of ice resting on each palm. If Elsa squinted hard, they looked like ice cubes that were just the right size for the teacups. She dropped them into the cups as Anna begged, 'Again!'

Elsa clamped her eyes shut and thought about ice cubes once more, but something else burst forth in her hands unexpectedly. It was small and lumpy, but she had made a snowball! Elsa held it out for her sister to see.

'Can I touch it?' Anna asked.

'Of course!' Elsa said.

Anna grabbed the snowball and tossed it in the air. She rolled it around in her hands as if she was testing it. Then she got a mischievous glint in her eye and Elsa could tell what she was thinking. Elsa ducked out of the fort just before Anna could throw the snowball in her direction.

'You can't get me!' Elsa called out. But there was nowhere to hide from Anna, because their little bedroom had been overtaken by the fort.

Elsa ducked into a hallway closet but regretted it. Anna would be waiting for her when she came out, Elsa suspected and she was right. The moment Elsa peered out of the closet, she felt the snowball splat against her cheek.

Fortunately, she knew how to make another one. *If* her magic behaved as she hoped.

Elsa came out of the closet, acting like their snowball fight was over.

'Let's go back into the fort,' she said to her sister. Anna looked at her suspiciously, but Elsa just said, 'What?' Anyone could see that her hands were empty.

Anna led the way inside the fort, settling down next to the dolls. Elsa picked up Hildy and gently gave her a sip of pretend tea, which was really a few drops of melted ice. Then, just when Anna was starting to relax into the fort's pillows, Elsa closed her eyes and focused on forming another snowball. It took a little more effort, but when she was done she noticed that the snowball she had made was a little firmer, more ice than snow.

'Oh, no you don't!' Anna yelled when she realised what her sister was doing. She grabbed the snowball and lobbed it at Elsa. There was a quick scuffle in the enclosed space of the fort, the sisters batting the snowball back and forth like a real ball until it fell from the air with a thud.

Right onto the snow hare plate Elsa had smuggled into the tent.

Breaking it in two.

Chapter 6
The Snow Hare

For Elsa, it felt like time had stopped. She picked up the two pieces of the plate and thought about how it had looked just seconds before. The snow hare had been hopping without a care in the world and now he was split in half. How had things gone so wrong so fast? The plate was ruined and it could never be fixed.

Or could it? Could her magic solve this problem? If only she could freeze the pieces back together . . . Elsa tried to use her magic, imagining ice that would connect the two broken sides. But it was as difficult as if she'd never had magic in the first place. Was her power as broken as the plate?

As she stared at the broken plate in her hands, she felt a warm stream of tears pouring down her face. Anna, who noticed Elsa had begun crying, wrapped her arms around her and said, 'It's okay. It's going to be okay.'

Ignoring Anna's words, Elsa shook

herself free of her sister's embrace and burst out of the fort. Anna meant well, but she didn't understand. The plates were part of the kingdom's history, of the knowledge Elsa was supposed to gain to become queen. How would she ever explain this to her parents?

Elsa wiped away her tears, a look of determination coming over her features. She would have to face the consequences. The sooner she admitted her mistake, the better.

Somehow, she pulled herself together. She changed out of her nightgown and went down the stairs and into the garden. She would own up to what she had done and accept any punishment. She would be as cold as ice.

But her courage melted away as soon as she stepped outside and saw her parents sitting in the shade of an elm tree. 'Oh, Mama,' she cried, running towards her. 'I am so sorry!' She crumpled to the ground by Queen Iduna.

Anna was right behind Elsa and she explained what had happened. 'Elsa borrowed the special plates for a tea party. And then we had a snowball fight . . . and one of them got broken.'

King Agnarr's eyes grew wide. 'A snowball fight?' he asked.

'I started it with my magic,' Elsa said. 'It's all my fault! I borrowed the plates, I made the snowballs and I ruined the snow hare.' She still had the pieces of the plate in her hand and she put them together to show her parents. 'He'll never be the same again.'

Queen Iduna pulled both of her daughters into her lap. 'Shhh . . . shhh.' She soothed Elsa, stroking her hair. 'Everything will be all right.'

'But it won't!' Elsa wailed. 'A little piece of the kingdom has been broken. By someone who is supposed to be the queen!' That was the worst part of it all. How could she be entrusted with such a huge responsibility when she couldn't even take care of a plate? Maybe she would *never* be ready to rule a kingdom.

Queen Iduna turned Elsa's face towards her and wiped away her tears. 'It will be many years before you are expected to take the throne,' she reassured her daughter. 'Nobody expects you to be perfect now. You are only learning. And one of the ways we learn is by making mistakes.'

Elsa sniffled. She did not like making mistakes and no matter what her mother said, she knew this was a big one. She took a deep breath. 'But now no-one will know the legend of the snow hare,' she said. She swallowed hard and willed herself not to cry anymore.

'Only the plate is broken,' King Agnarr reassured her. 'Not the story! The legend is much more important than the plate itself. And it will live in Arendelle forever.'

From the other side of the queen's lap, Anna piped up. 'What's the legend of the snow hare?'

Queen Iduna leaned back and paused,

as if summoning a precious memory. 'The snow hare lives in the woods and fields of Arendelle, blending in with his surroundings all winter long,' she said.

'And he is magic?' Anna asked.

Elsa smiled, though her eyes still felt a little puffy. Of course Anna wanted to know about the magic.

'Some say,' added the king, 'that the snow hare can bring a person good luck for a lifetime.'

Anna's eyes widened. 'How does he do that?' she asked.

'All you have to do is hold the snow hare in your arms,' the queen explained. 'But that is easier said than done, because he is almost impossible to catch. He lives in the open, so people may spot him in the woods or fields in summertime. He may even come close, daring us to catch him. In the end, though, the snow hare darts away. He always manages to keep his good luck to himself.'

'That's no fair,' Anna said. 'The snow hare should share his magic with everyone.'

But Elsa saw the story differently. Magic could work wonders, but she knew why the snow hare would guard his carefully. Because magic could also be too powerful to control. And when it slipped out of your hands, it could even be a little dangerous.

Chapter 7
The Perfect Summer Night

By the end of their first week at the Sommerhus, the broken plate was just an ache in the back of Elsa's mind, something she could almost forget. She was still in her favourite place with her favourite people and nothing could ruin that.

One night, near sunset, Anna and Elsa went to the edge of the woods to look for kindling for a fire while Queen Iduna stood nearby. They scampered along the hiking path, piling sticks and pieces of bark into baskets they carried and playing their usual game. 'Don't touch the ground!' Elsa said, hopping from root to root. 'Anna, you're slipping . . .' Her sister had one foot on a rock and one on a rickety log.

Anna's gaze was fixed on something deep in the woods. 'Shhh,' she told her sister, putting a finger to her lips. 'I think I see the snow hare!' She pointed into the distance and Elsa stepped in that direction.

'You touched the ground!' said Anna. 'I win this round!'

Elsa frowned. 'Were you tricking me?'

she asked. 'Did you really see the snow hare at all?'

Anna shook her head. 'Okay, I made it up,' she admitted. 'Because you always win the game.'

'I'm older,' Elsa said, standing up straight and sticking her chin out.

'And someday you'll be queen,' replied Anna, sweeping into a curtsy.

Elsa did not want to think about being queen or imagine what the next day's lessons would bring. In the past few days, she had learned how to write official letters and how to call for the royal guards.

'Don't touch the ground!' she cautioned

her sister, moving up the path and starting the game again. She just wanted to enjoy her time at the Sommerhus, where worries seemed to vanish in the breeze that fanned the fjord.

When their mother led them back to the cottage, King Agnarr was building the fire. He took the kindling from their baskets, feeding the flames until the family's bonfire lit up the early evening. As the sun sank lower in the sky, the fire grew bolder and brighter, crackling with life.

Beside the fire, Anna bounced in anticipation. 'When are we roasting marshmallows?'

'Right now!' said Queen Iduna, carrying a bowl full of marshmallows to the fire. Elsa put one on the end of her stick and roasted it patiently. She waited to eat her marshmallow until it was golden brown all around.

Anna, on the other hand, strung five marshmallows along her stick and stuck it into the hottest part of the flames. Soon, her marshmallows were black on the outside and raw on the inside, but she didn't care one bit. She tugged them from her stick one-by-one and devoured them in seconds. As soon as she had finished them, she asked, 'Can I have some more?'

'Not tonight,' said King Agnarr. His face was lit by the soft glow from the fire. Their father reached down and lifted one of his fiddles to his chin. Keeping time by tapping his toes, the king began to play one of their favourite tunes.

Anna and Elsa sprang up to twirl in circles around the fire, their favourite kind of dancing. And then, when they were tired after a dozen songs, they lay on the grass and watched the twinkling stars.

Elsa imagined connecting the stars to form the shape of a rabbit and thought some more about the snow hare. Why would she need his good luck anyway? Maybe she could use it in the future. Good luck might help her master her magic. Maybe it would even help her when she became the queen. Too bad no-one ever caught the snow hare. It was sad he was only a legend.

When the fire died down, it was time for the girls to go to bed. They ducked into their fort and checked on Hildy and Hanna before snuggling into bed. Queen Iduna sat with one arm around each of her daughters as she read them fairy tales; then she tucked them in for the night.

'Sweet dreams,' she said. 'Tomorrow will be a new adventure!'

The room was dark when their mother left and shadows moved across the ceiling. Next to Elsa, Anna propped herself up on one elbow. 'Want to tell ghost stories?' she asked.

Elsa could already hear the wind howling through the trees. It did sound a little like ghosts, she thought. 'Sure!'

She was careful not to make her story too scary for Anna, though. Hers was about a friendly ghost who returned to the same

cottage summer after summer to visit the place he loved the most.

Anna's story was darker and more dramatic. 'This is about the ghosts of the people who looked for the snow hare but never found him,' she began. 'They never found good luck. Actually, all their luck was bad . . .'

Elsa couldn't let Anna give herself nightmares. 'Let's save that one for tomorrow night, okay?' she said. She hugged her sister and closed her eyes, pretending to sleep.

In no time, Anna was breathing evenly, lost to the world of dreams. Elsa wasn't tired yet, but she knew a good way to put herself to sleep. All Elsa needed to do was start reviewing her list of Arendelle's rulers and she drifted off at once.

In the middle of the night, though, Elsa awoke with a start. For a moment she forgot where she was, but soon she remembered.

Their little room, the summer, the fort, the dolls, the plate, the future. But something wasn't right.

Elsa was still half asleep, so it took a moment for her foggy mind to realise what was wrong.

The spot beside her in bed was warm, but her sister wasn't there.

Chapter 8
Chasing Anna

Elsa blinked. Maybe Anna had gone downstairs for a drink of water or a midnight snack. Maybe she was with their parents, or somewhere else in the Sommerhus.

Elsa wouldn't be able to sleep until she knew, so she rolled out of bed and stretched. Lots of people woke up in the middle of the night, Elsa told herself. Anna's usual way at the Sommerhus was to go to bed late and wake up at the crack of dawn, but that didn't mean she couldn't break her pattern. Maybe nothing was wrong at all.

It was possible. But Elsa had a bad feeling.

She ran her hands along the other side of the bed to make sure her sister wasn't huddled under the blankets. Anna wasn't there.

Elsa slipped out of the room. Should she wake her parents? She did not want them to worry. For now, at least, she decided to search for Anna by herself.

Elsa tiptoed downstairs. The glow of moonlight washed over everything, but the corners were dark and the grandfather clock cast an ominous shadow. Elsa darted into each room, scanning for Anna. 'Come out, come out, wherever you are,' she whispered, but no-one answered.

Would Anna have left the Sommerhus? Most kids wouldn't dare go outside at

night alone, but Elsa knew her sister. Anna was fearless and bold, a girl who wouldn't let anything get between her and her next big idea.

But why? What could Anna want outside? Elsa had no answers, but she knew that Anna shouldn't be alone. She was too little and it was too dark. Her skin prickled with goose bumps.

Elsa opened the door, taking care not to make any noise and propped it open with a stone so she could get back in without waking her parents. There was no need to worry them, she decided. Anna couldn't have gone very far.

Stepping outside, Elsa crisscrossed the gardens of the Sommerhus, softly calling, 'Anna? Anna? Are you out there?' But there was only silence.

When a cloud drifted over the moon, the grounds around the cottage turned pitch black. In another section of sky, the stars still winked, so Elsa would have to rely on their dim light to see.

She took a deep breath. Where was she going to go?

Elsa thought again about waking her parents but decided to put it off a little longer. Any minute, she expected to find her sister.

She walked along the edge of the gardens and spotted Anna's cloak near the hiking path. Had she worn it outside, then grown too warm? She had to be close, Elsa thought.

Anna probably wasn't scared, but Elsa shivered as she hurried along the path. Wasn't her father always cautioning against the dangers of the woods? Elsa's imagination ran wild. There could be animals out there, hungry and fierce. There could even be monsters. And Elsa knew that a person could get lost among the trees without anyone ever realising they were there.

That was the most frightening thing, Elsa thought—being alone. And thinking of Anna alone, in danger.

Elsa paused for a moment to calm her racing heart and when she stopped she remembered something: Anna might be alone, but Elsa didn't need to be. Elsa had magic to keep her company.

Her worries made the magic difficult to manage at first. After a few misshapen lumps, though, Elsa finally conjured something that resembled a snowball. Its cold weight in her hands felt reassuring; every time she felt a new surge of worry, she squeezed it to relieve the pressure. Soon the snowball was dented and melting, but Elsa's spirits were restored. Anna couldn't have gone that far, Elsa told herself. Any minute, she would find her.

As she rushed ahead, Elsa's eyes tried to take in every inch of the trail. Strangely, she was getting used to the dark and as time went on it seemed almost like the forest was allowing her to see things she had never noticed before.

The wind had been howling, but now it tickled Elsa's nose, teasing her like a friend. Leaves rose in a gust and it looked like they were dancing. Even the taste of the air was sharp and fresh, like lemon or mint. Was this why her mother loved the outdoors so much? Maybe these natural wonders were the true treasures of the kingdom.

Elsa was almost at the top of a hill, which ended at a bluff. She could hear the gentle lapping of water far below. Would Anna have gone down there? Elsa panicked. Could she have been swept out to sea? She squeezed her snowball for comfort, digging her fingernails into its cold centre and then she remembered what Anna had said. The water was too cold. She wouldn't even walk into it. She wouldn't have come this way, Elsa thought. She could feel it in her bones.

She turned around on the trail and headed back the way she had come, relieved to sense Anna wasn't in the water but frustrated that there was still no sign of her sister. If only she had woken her parents at once! She needed help and she was too far into the forest to turn back. For the hundredth time, Elsa wondered what Anna was thinking. Why was she out there at all?

Elsa was walking near the strawberry bushes, feeling her way past a row of pines, when suddenly she heard a faint voice. Was it the wind? Was it just her imagination?

She wasn't sure until she finally made out the words.

'Elsa, come! I found him! I found the snow hare!'

Chapter 9
A Rescue

Elsa froze in place. It was Anna.

Her voice was louder now. 'Elsa! I'm over here!' she said. 'I knew you would find me.'

Elsa's eyes scanned the forest, but she could barely see beyond the trees in front of her.

'Help me!' Anna called. 'I'm stuck!'

Elsa moved towards Anna's voice, keeping

her arms out in front of her so she would not crash into anything. She knew that her sister was nearby, but she wanted to *see* her.

'Help!' Anna cried out again.

Elsa looked up, scanning the treetops, but it was only when she looked down that she understood the problem. She gasped. Only a few steps ahead of her, hidden by shadow and brush, was a deep hole. In the dark, she could barely make out Anna sitting at the bottom.

'I found him, Elsa!' Anna said.

Elsa was confused until she caught sight of her sister's eyes, which were lit with excitement. And her sister's arms, which were full of something white and fluffy and kicking furiously.

Elsa took a cautious step backwards. 'What is that?' she asked.

'I told you!' Anna exclaimed. 'It's the snow hare!' Now Elsa could see that the white fluff had long ears and a puffy tail. It was larger than any rabbit she had ever seen, but otherwise it looked perfectly normal.

Whether or not it was the legendary bunny, Anna struggled to keep hold of it. 'I followed him down here, but now we're stuck. You have to help us out!' she said.

Elsa walked closer to the edge of the hole

and peered down. Someone must have been digging there, maybe to plant or to build something. The hole was deep and wide enough to hold their room in the Sommerhus.

'Oh, Anna . . .' said Elsa. Her sister was asking her to do something that seemed impossible. 'The hole is huge!' She didn't want to scare Anna, but she had to be honest. 'I don't know how to get you out.'

'It's not just me,' Anna reminded her, 'but also the snow hare. He's coming with me! I saw him outside the cottage from our window and followed him all the way here.' She sounded quite proud of herself.

Elsa sighed. She was pretty sure it was

just a regular rabbit. But when Anna got an idea into her head, it was hard to talk her out of it. 'Yes, and the snow hare,' she agreed. There was no point in fighting about it.

She stretched her arm out to Anna. 'I can't reach!' Anna said, extending her own arm as far as it would go. Her fingers grazed Elsa's, but she was too far away to grab it.

'I have a better idea,' Elsa said. 'I think you have to run and jump to reach my hands.'

Anna tried jumping once and then again, but she lost her footing and landed back at the bottom of the hole. She fell on her back and the rabbit wiggled free from her grasp. In a flash, he scrambled up the

side of the hole and disappeared into the darkness.

Anna began to cry. 'Noooo!' she wailed. 'He was supposed to bring us good luck!'

'Shhh, Anna, don't cry,' Elsa said, trying to sound calm. 'I will get you out of there!' She just had to think for a minute. She sat down at the top of the hole, careful not to fall in herself.

Elsa frowned, feeling hopeless. Someday, a whole kingdom would be hers, but what good would that be if she couldn't even rescue her sister? She didn't have the power to do the one thing she wanted to do the most.

Elsa sat up straight. That was it.

She did have power – the power of her magic.

True, her magic could be trouble, like when it led to her breaking the plate. It could be unpredictable. But when it worked right, it could let her do almost anything.

Maybe even save her sister.

'I'm cold,' Anna piped up. 'It's dark down here.'

Elsa stood and forced herself to sound cheerful. 'Think of it like our fort,' she said. 'It's your own special hideout! You're perfectly fine in there for now.' Elsa did not want Anna to lose hope. She did not want her sister to doubt what she was about to try next.

Anna sniffled and put her head in her hands. 'I miss Hildy and Hanna.'

'You'll be seeing them in no time,' Elsa assured her. If she could get her magic to do exactly what she wanted, that was. It was a big *if*, but she had to try.

Elsa closed her eyes and summoned her power. She would need more than snowballs or icicles. Taking in a deep breath, Elsa concentrated harder than she ever had before.

She'd conjured up a sheet of ice. Could she make stairs? A rope? A slide?

After a few minutes of intense focus, she heard Anna's reaction from below.

'Oh!' she said. 'I'm skating!' Without realising it, Elsa had spread a thin layer of ice around the bottom of the hole.

'Sorry!' said Elsa. 'Let me try again.' That was not quite what she had meant to do. 'Anna, can you step off the ice for a second?'

Elsa stared below and concentrated hard. Stairs would be too difficult, she decided. A rope was too likely to break. But what about a ramp? That meant Elsa had to come up with a sheet of ice that would stretch from the bottom of the hole to the top, where she stood, plus be strong enough to hold Anna. If it broke, Anna would fall.

This was more than Elsa had ever asked of her magic before and her instinct was to scrunch herself up to control it. Unless . . . would it be better to let her powers go? At once, Elsa knew what to do. She flung her arms out and let magic pour from her fingertips.

She did not dare to look, but Anna told her what she needed to know.

'There's a ramp, Elsa,' Anna said with wonder. 'Can I walk on it?'

How long would this burst of power last? Elsa finally glanced down at the ramp she was building. It was hard to make out in the dark, but she could see the uneven slope of snow and ice inching to the top of the hole.

'Yes!' Elsa said, once the ramp was long enough for Anna to get out. 'But it's very slippery! Please be careful, okay? And hurry! I don't know how long we have.'

Elsa's heart felt still as her magic kept flowing. She was almost frozen with fear, until she saw Anna emerge from the hole.

Her sister was fine and it didn't matter that the magic was beginning to fade. Elsa was brave, and Anna was safe; and if they were really lucky, they could get back to the Sommerhus before sunrise.

Chapter 10
A New Day

The first hints of dawn spread across the sky as the sisters walked back home. Anna was unusually quiet and Elsa was lost in thought. How would they explain to their parents what had happened? Even if they might get in trouble, Elsa wanted her mum and dad to know how she had used her magic to help Anna. It was a good sign for the future, she thought. Maybe someday she'd have full control over her power!

Control over her little sister was another story, she thought. Turning to Anna, Elsa said, 'What were you thinking, sneaking out like that? Something terrible could have happened.'

'Something terrible *did* happen,' Anna pointed out. 'But you saved me, just like I knew you would.'

Elsa had to smile. Her sister had so much faith in her.

'I woke up in the middle of the night,' Anna explained, 'and I was thinking about our ghost stories. And then, from the window, I could see a bunny. I knew it was the snow hare! I just had to chase him. What if I never got another chance to catch his good luck?'

'What do you need good luck for?' Elsa asked.

'No, no, it wasn't for me,' explained Anna. 'The good luck was supposed to be for you.'

'For me?' Elsa asked. She looked at Anna in surprise. She didn't understand.

'To help you when you become queen,' Anna said. 'I thought you could use a little extra luck. Just in case.'

Elsa's heart warmed. She didn't need good luck when she had a sister like Anna. Her sister might be the kindest girl in the whole world, she thought.

'I'm sorry you lost the snow hare,' Elsa said, hugging Anna.

'It's okay,' replied Anna. 'I'll find him again someday, I just know it.'

Did her sister even understand the difference between real life and legends? There was no such thing as a snow hare, or at least not one that could change your life forever. But there was no convincing Anna, so Elsa just smiled and said, 'I hope you do.'

When they reached the Sommerhus, they tugged open the door and listened carefully. They couldn't hear their parents at all. They were still in bed!

'Let's make them breakfast!' Anna said.

But her idea of breakfast was more like dessert. Elsa didn't have the heart to tell her that no-one else would want to eat a bowl of strawberries stuck together with syrup and chocolate.

Elsa set the table with her mother's

special plates and sat down with her parents after they had come downstairs rubbing their eyes.

'What is this?' asked King Agnarr. 'A party?'

Elsa and Anna nodded. Before Elsa could explain why they were awake so early, Anna beat her to it.

'We went on an adventure!' her little sister exclaimed.

The king and queen were not happy to hear of their daughters' nighttime outing.

'The forest can be dangerous,' King Agnarr pointed out, as he had many times before. 'Anything could have happened and we would never have known where to look for you.'

But the king and queen were happy to eat the strawberries – or they acted happy, anyway – and happy to hear that Elsa's magic had saved Anna from the hole in the woods.

'The magic did exactly what you asked?' said Queen Iduna. She put an arm around Elsa and hugged her. 'I'm so proud of you!'

Those words were music to Elsa's ears and after hearing them she did not even mind washing the dishes. For the next few days, their parents said, the girls would be doing some extra work around the cottage to make up for leaving the house without permission in the middle of the night.

Soon, it was time for Elsa to go back to her lessons. She got a lump in her throat when Anna left to play outside and she was stuck studying an old book about Arendelle's best-known artists and musicians. It took Elsa a while to settle into it, but after she did, she saw what made those people special. They might not have had magic, but they were clever and resourceful, bold and courageous.

'You did a brave thing, helping your sister,' Queen Iduna said as Elsa finished the last chapter of her book. She leaned over

and put a hand on Elsa's shoulder, giving it a gentle squeeze. 'You are going to make a great leader someday.'

Elsa smiled at her mum, the queen's words filling her with warmth. She had always worried her magic would make it harder to be a good queen, but maybe her power didn't make her so different from the rulers of the past after all.

'I think you've read enough for today,' said Queen Iduna. 'You're free to go and play with Anna.'

Elsa put down her book and raced outside to look for Anna, but there was no sign of her sister. Not again!

'Have you seen Anna anywhere?' she asked her father.

King Agnarr looked up from the book he was reading and said, 'I just saw her, but I think she must have gone inside.'

Taking the stairs two at a time, Elsa ran to their room and pushed open the door. When she didn't spot Anna, she knew her sister had to be in the fort.

'Hello, girls,' she said to Hildy and Hanna, who were by the window. Then she peeked inside the fort. 'Anna?' she said. It was strangely quiet in there.

'Shhh,' Anna whispered. 'He's sleeping.'

Elsa wasn't sure if it was lucky or unlucky, but her sister never gave up on anything. She must have been searching all morning, Elsa realised, but she'd finally found what she wanted.

Curled up on Anna's lap was a large white rabbit. 'The rest of our summer will be perfect,' she predicted with a grin. 'Because I finally caught the snow hare.'